BENEATH
A TRAVELLING
STAR

Thirty contemporary carols and hymns for Christmas

TIMOTHY DUDLEY-SMITH

Music Editor: Lionel Dakers
Music Engraver: Andrew Parker

CANTERBURY
PRESS
Norwich

Hope Publishing Company

CONTENTS

*For my wife Arlette, Caroline and David, Sarah and Giles, James and Becky,
and for Jonathan and Susanna: with all who shared our family Christmas over
more than forty years in The Drive, at Rectory Meadow, and at Ashlands*

1   A new song God has given

CRÜGER   76 76 D

Adapted from Johann Crüger 1598–1662
by W. H. Monk 1823–1889

alternative tune MORNING LIGHT

A NEW song God has given,
   a new thing God has done,
when from the courts of heaven
   he sent to us his Son.
Rejoice in song and story
   to tell of Jesus' birth,
who laid aside his glory
   and came, a child, to earth.

2 A new-born baby sleeping,
      a mother's tender care,
   while ox and ass are keeping
      their night-long vigil there;
   to greet the infant stranger
      the shepherds make their way,
   to find, within a manger,
      the child of Christmas Day.

3 A new-found star is shining
      upon the eastern skies,
   that kings may come, divining
      the way of all the wise.
   O child of our salvation,
      receive the gifts we bring,
   the songs of adoration
      that love alone can sing.

4 A new world now is waking,
      the old must pass away;
   a new-made morning breaking
      on God's eternal day.
   A new song God has given
      to tell his praise abroad,
   who came, a child, from heaven,
      a Saviour, Christ the Lord.

2   A song was heard at Christmas

ALFORD   76 86 86 86

J. B. Dykes 1823–1876

alternative tune CHERRY TREE CAROL

A SONG was heard at Christmas
   to wake the midnight sky:
a Saviour's birth, and peace on earth,
   and praise to God on high.
The angels sang at Christmas
   with all the hosts above,
and still we sing the newborn King,
   his glory and his love.

2   A star was seen at Christmas,
     a herald and a sign,
that all might know the way to go
   to find the child divine.
The wise men watched at Christmas
   in some far eastern land,
and still the wise in starry skies
   discern their Maker's hand.

3   A tree was grown at Christmas,
     a sapling green and young;
no tinsel bright with candlelight
   upon its branches hung.
But he who came at Christmas
   our sins and sorrows bore,
and still we name his tree of shame
   our life for evermore.

4   A child was born at Christmas
     when Christmas first began;
the Lord of all a baby small,
   the Son of God made man.
For love is ours at Christmas,
   and life and light restored,
and so we praise through endless days
   the Saviour, Christ the Lord.

3   Child of Mary, newly born

LYNCH'S LULLABY   77 77 D

Irish cradle song from
J. P. Lynch's *Melodies of Ireland* c. 1845
arranged by Donald Davison b. 1937

alternative tune HOLLINGSIDE

CHILD of Mary, newly born,
    softly in a manger laid,
wake to wonder on this morn,
    view the world your fingers made.
Starlight shone above your bed,
    lantern-light about your birth:
morning sunlight crown your head,
    light and life of all the earth!

2   Child of Mary, grown and strong,
        traveller, teacher, young and free,
    see him stride the hills along,
        Christ the Man of Galilee.
    Wisdom from a world above
        now by waiting hearts is heard:
    hear him speak the words of love,
        Christ the true eternal Word,

3   Child of Mary, grief and loss,
        all the sum of human woe,
    crown of thorn and cruel cross,
        mark the path you choose to go.
    Man of sorrows, born to save,
        bearing all our sins and pains:
    from his cross and empty grave
        Christ the Lord of glory reigns.

4   Child of Mary, gift of grace,
        by whose birth shall all be well,
    one with us in form and face,
        God with us, Emmanuel!
    Night is past and shadows fled,
        wake to joy on Christmas morn:
    sunlight crown the Saviour's head,
        Christ the Prince of peace is born.

Arrangement © 1991 Oxford University Press, Great Clarendon Street, Oxford OX2 6DP
from *New Songs of Praise 6*, used by permission.
Text © Copyright Timothy Dudley-Smith in Europe (including UK and Ireland) and Africa,
and in the rest of the world © 1993 by Hope Publishing Company

4   Child of the stable's secret birth

NEWTOWN ST LUKE   89 99 98

Anthony Caesar *b.* 1924

UNISON   *Verses 2 & 4 may be sung with wordless harmony.*

1 Child of the sta - - - ble's se - - cret birth, the
2 Eyes__ that shine in the lan - - tern's ray; a
3 Voice__ that rang through the courts on high con -
4 In - - fant hands in a mo - - ther's hand, for
5 Child of the sta - - - ble's se - - cret birth, the

Lord by right of the lords of earth, let
face so small in its nest of hay,_____
- tract - ed now to a word - less cry, a
none but Ma - ry may un - - der - stand_____
Fa - ther's gift to a way - - ward earth, to

an - - gels sing of a King new - born, the
face of a child who is born to scan the
voice__ to mas - - ter the wind and wave, the
whose are the hands and the fin - - gers curled but
drain__ the cup in a few short years of

Music © Canterbury Press Norwich, St Mary's Works, St Mary's Plain, Norwich NR3 3BH

world   is   weav-ing   a   crown   of   thorn: a
world   he made through the   eyes   of   man: and
hu - - man heart and   the   hun - - gry grave: the
his   who fa - shioned and made   our world;   and
all   our sor - rows, our sins   and tears;_____

crown   of thorn for that in - - fant head
from   that face in the   fi - - nal day
voice   of God through the ce - - dar trees
through   these hands in the hour   of death
ours   the prize for the road   he trod:

cra - - dled soft   in the   man - - ger bed.
earth__   and heav - en shall flee__   a - way.
rol - - ling forth   as the   sound_   of seas.
nails__   shall strike to the wood_   be - neath.
ri - sen   with Christ;__ at   peace_   with God.

5 Chill of the nightfall

BUNESSAN   10 9 10 9

Gaelic melody
arranged by Noël Tredinnick b. 1949

CHILL of the nightfall,
lamps in the windows,
letting their light fall
clear on the snow;
    bitter December
    bids us remember
Christ in the stable
long, long ago.

2 Silence of midnight,
voices of angels,
singing to bid night
yield to the dawn;
    darkness is ended,
    sinners befriended,
where in the stable
Jesus is born.

3 Splendour of starlight
high on the hillside,
faint is the far light
burning below;
    kneeling before him
    shepherds adore him,
Christ in the stable
long, long ago.

4 Glory of daybreak!
Sorrows and shadows,
suddenly they break
forth into morn;
    sing out and tell now
    all shall be well now,
for in the stable
Jesus is born!

6   Christ is come! Let earth adore him

Lux Eoi   87 87 D   Arthur Sullivan 1842–1900

alternative tunes   ABBOT'S LEIGH, HYFRYDOL

CHRIST is come! Let earth adore him;
    God appears in mortal frame.
Saints and angels bow before him,
    praise his high and holy Name.
Word of our salvation's story,
    helpless babe of human birth,
Christ has laid aside his glory,
    born for us a child of earth.

2   Christ is come and calls us to him;
        here by faith behold your King;
    with the shepherds kneel to view him,
        with the wise your treasures bring.
    Child today and man tomorrow,
        by his cross and crown of thorn
    he shall vanquish sin and sorrow,
        sing we then that Christ is born.

3   Christ is come! Let all enthrone him,
        every tongue declare his praise;
    every heart rejoice to own him
        King of everlasting days.
    Christ is come, our sure salvation,
        Christ the ransomed sinner's friend,
    so with all his new creation
        sing the song that knows no end.

7   Come now with awe

FINLANDIA   11 10 11 10 11 10

from *Finlandia* by
Jean Sibelius 1865–1957

COME now with awe, earth's ancient vigil keeping;
cold under starlight lies the stony way.
Down from the hillside see the shepherds creeping,
hear in our hearts the whispered news they say:
    'Laid in a manger lies an infant sleeping,
    Christ our Redeemer, born for us today.'

2   Come now with joy to worship and adore him;
hushed in the stillness, wonder and behold,
Christ in the stable where his mother bore him,
Christ whom the prophets faithfully foretold:
    High King of ages, low we kneel before him,
    starlight for silver, lantern-light for gold.

3   Come now with faith, the age-long secret guessing,
hearts rapt in wonder, soul and spirit stirred;
see in our likeness love beyond expressing,
all God has spoken, all the prophets heard;
    born for us sinners, bearer of all blessing,
    flesh of our flesh, behold the eternal Word!

4   Come now with love; beyond our comprehending
love in its fulness lies in mortal span!
How should we love, whom Love is so befriending?
Love rich in mercy since our race began
    now stoops to save us, sighs and sorrows ending,
    Jesus our Saviour, Son of God made man.

Music © Breitkopf & Härtel, Walkmühlstraße 52, D-65195 Wiesbaden, Germany
Used by permission

Text © Copyright Timothy Dudley-Smith in Europe (including UK and Ireland) and Africa,
and in the rest of the world © 1983 by Hope Publishing Company

8   Come, watch with us

KINGSFOLD   DCM

English folksong from *English Country Songs* 1893
harmonised by Ralph Vaughan Williams 1872–1958

alternative tunes COE FEN, SOLL 'S SEIN, THE AULD HOOSE

COME, watch with us this Christmas night;
our hearts must travel far
to darkened hills and heavens bright
with star on shining star;
to where in shadowy silence sleep
the fields of Bethlehem,
as shepherds wake their watch to keep
and we will watch with them.

2   Who would not join the angel songs
that tell the Saviour's birth?
The Lord for whom creation longs
has come at last to earth;
the fulness of the Father's love
is ours at Bethlehem,
while angels throng the skies above
and we will sing with them.

3   Who would not journey far to share
the wisdom of the wise,
and gaze with them in wonder where
the world's Redeemer lies?
The Lord of all the lords that are
is born at Bethlehem,
and kings shall kneel beneath his star
and we will bow with them.

4   Lift every heart the hymn of praise
that all creation sings;
the angel host its homage pays,
the shepherds and the kings.
For earth and sky with one accord,
O Child of Bethlehem,
are come to worship Christ the Lord
and we will come with them.

9 Donkey plod and Mary ride

ENGLANDS LANE   77 77 and refrain

English melody
adapted by Geoffrey Shaw 1879–1943

DONKEY plod and Mary ride,
weary Joseph walk beside,
theirs the way that all men come,
dark the night and far from home:
    down the years remember them,
    come away to Bethlehem.

2   Mary's child, on Christmas Eve,
    none but ox and ass receive;
    theirs the manger and the stall
    where is laid the Lord of all:
        down the years remember them,
        come away to Bethlehem.

3   Angels throng the midnight sky:
    'Glory be to God on high'.
    Theirs the song that sounds abroad,
    'Born a Saviour, Christ the Lord':
        down the years remember them,
        come away to Bethlehem.

4   Shepherds haste the watch to keep
    where their Maker lies asleep;
    theirs the angels' promised sign,
    'Born for us a child divine':
        down the years remember them,
        come away to Bethlehem.

5   Ancient kings from eastern skies
    trace the way of all the wise,
    theirs the shining star, to find
    light to lighten all mankind:
        down the years remember them,
        come away to Bethlehem.

6   Shepherds, kings and angel throngs,
    teach us where our joy belongs;
    souls restored and sins forgiven,
    Christ on earth the hope of heaven:
        down the years rejoice in them,
        come away to Bethlehem.

10 Had he not loved us

ELLERS   10 10 10 10

E. J. Hopkins 1818–1901
reharmonised by Arthur Sullivan 1842–1900

alternative tune ANIMA CHRISTI

HAD he not loved us
    he had never come,
yet is he love
    and love is all his way;
low to the mystery
    of the virgin's womb
Christ bows his glory,
    born on Christmas Day.

2   Had he not loved us
        he had never come;
    had he not come
        he need have never died,
    nor won the victory
        of the vacant tomb,
    the awful triumph
        of the Crucified.

3   Had he not loved us
        he had never come;
    still were we lost
        in sorrow, sin and shame,
    the doors fast shut
        on our eternal home
    which now stand open,
        for he loved and came.

11   Hear how the bells of Christmas play!

LASST UNS ERFREUEN 88 44 88 and Alleluias
(EASTER SONG)

Melody from an Easter hymn
in *Geistliche Kirchengesang* Cologne 1623
arranged by Ralph Vaughan Williams 1872–1958

O__ praise him! Al - le - lu - ia.

O__ praise him! O__ praise him! Al - le -

- lu - ia, al - le - lu - ia, al - le - lu - - ia.

HEAR how the bells of Christmas play!
Well may they ring for joy and say,
    O praise him! Alleluia!
God has fulfilled his promised word,
born is our Saviour and our Lord,
    O praise him! Alleluia!

2   Let all the waiting earth rejoice,
    lift every heart and every voice,
        O praise him! Alleluia!
    Sing now the song to angels given,
    Glory to God in highest heaven!
        O praise him! Alleluia!

3   As through the silence of the skies
    shepherds in wonder heard arise,
        O praise him! Alleluia!
    So may we hear again with them
    songs in the night at Bethlehem,
        O praise him! Alleluia!

4   All nature sang at Jesus' birth,
    hail the Creator come to earth!
        O praise him! Alleluia!
    Sun, moon and shining stars above,
    tell out the story of his love,
        O praise him! Alleluia!

5   Hear how the bells of Christmas play!
    Well may they ring for joy and say,
        O praise him! Alleluia!
    Come now to worship and adore,
    Christ is our peace for evermore,
        O praise him! Alleluia!

12   Here is the centre: star on distant star

Song 1   10 10 10 10 10 10   Orlando Gibbons 1583–1625

HERE is the centre: star on distant star
shining unheeded in the depths of space,
worlds without number, all the worlds there are,
turn in their travelling to this holy place.
 Here in a stable and an ox's stall
 laid in a manger lies the Lord of all.

2 Now is the moment: God in flesh appears,
down from the splendours of his throne sublime,
High King of Ages, Lord of all the years,
God everlasting stoops to space and time.
 All that was promised now is brought to birth,
 Jesus our Saviour come at last to earth.

3 Son of the Father, God's eternal Word,
emptied of glory, born to cross and grave;
ours is the secret ancient prophets heard,
God in our likeness come to seek and save:
 Christ in his passion, bearer of our sins;
 and, from his rising, risen life begins.

4 Come then rejoicing! Praise be all our songs!
Love lies among us in the stable bare,
light in our darkness, righting of all wrongs,
hope for the future, joy enough to share.
 Peace to our hearts for God is on the throne!
 Christ our Redeemer comes to claim his own.

13   Holy child, how still you lie

HOLY CHILD   77 77 D

Michael Baughen *b.* 1930
arranged by Noël Tredinnick *b.* 1949

alternative tune BUCKLAND

Arrangement © Noël Tredinnick / Jubilate Hymns, Southwick House, 4 Thorne Park Road, Chelston, Torquay TQ2 6RX
Administered outside the UK by Hope Publishing Company

HOLY child, how still you lie!
    safe the manger, soft the hay;
faint upon the eastern sky
    breaks the dawn of Christmas Day.

2   Holy child, whose birthday brings
        shepherds from their field and fold,
    angel choirs and eastern kings,
        myrrh and frankincense and gold:

3   Holy child, what gift of grace
        from the Father freely willed!
    In your infant form we trace
        all God's promises fulfilled.

4   Holy child, whose human years
        span like ours delight and pain;
    one in human joys and tears,
        one in all but sin and stain:

5   Holy child, so far from home,
        all the lost to seek and save,
    to what dreadful death you come,
        to what dark and silent grave!

6   Holy child, before whose Name
        powers of darkness faint and fall;
    conquered, death and sin and shame,
        Jesus Christ is Lord of all!

7   Holy child, how still you lie!
        safe the manger, soft the hay;
    clear upon the eastern sky
        breaks the dawn of Christmas Day.

14 How faint the stable lantern's light

THIS ENDRIS NYGHT   CM

English 15th-century carol

alternative tunes BEATITUDO, ST BOTOLPH

HOW faint the stable-lantern's light
but in the east afar
upon the darkness burning bright
there shines a single star.

2 A homeless child is brought to birth,
yet love and faith shall find
a candle lit for all the earth,
the hope of humankind;

3 A flame to warm the barren hearth,
a lamp for all who roam,
to shine upon the heavenward path
and light our journey home.

15   How silent waits the listening earth

CoE FEN   DCM

Ken Naylor 1931–1991

alternative tunes KINGSFOLD, LADYWELL

HOW silent waits the listening earth
   beneath a cloud-dark sky,
no star to mark the midnight birth,
   the new-born baby's cry;
till angel voices lift their songs
   and glory shines abroad,
for him to whom all praise belongs,
   a Saviour, Christ the Lord.

2   On trembling feet, from flock and fold,
      the shepherds hasten down;
   the child of whom the angel told
      is born in David's town.
   They gaze in wide-eyed wonder there
      on Mary's child asleep,
   the Lamb of God, our sins to bear,
      the Shepherd of his sheep.

3   By mountain ways and deserts wide,
      from kingly courts afar,
   the wise men in their wisdom ride
      beneath a travelling star.
   Beyond the treasures wealth can buy,
      the truths by sages heard,
   there shines the wisdom from on high
      in God's incarnate Word.

4   To him whom now by faith we know
      with angel choirs we sing;
   and like the wise, so long ago,
      our treasures too we bring.
   O child, to whom the shepherds came
      and knelt to you alone,
   we name your everlasting Name,
      the Lamb upon his throne!

16   Hush you, my baby

Hushaby   55 65 D

melody Michael Baughen *b.* 1930
harmonised by Lionel Dakers *b.* 1924

HUSH you, my baby,
the night wind is cold,
the lambs from the hillside
are safe in the fold.
Sleep with the starlight
and wake with the morn,
    the Lord of all glory
a baby is born.

2 Hush you, my baby,
so soon to be grown,
watching by moonlight
on mountains alone,
toiling and travelling
so sleep while you can,
    till the Lord of all glory
is seen as a man.

3 Hush you, my baby,
the years will not stay;
the cross on the hilltop
the end of the way.
Dim through the darkness,
in grief and in gloom,
    the Lord of all glory
lies cold in the tomb.

4 Hush you, my baby,
the Father on high
in power and dominion
the darkness puts by;
bright from the shadows,
the seal and the stone,
    the Lord of all glory
returns to his own.

5 Hush you, my baby,
the sky turns to gold;
the lambs on the hillside
are loose from the fold;
fast fades the midnight
and new springs the morn,
    for the Lord of all glory
a Saviour is born.

17   In our darkness light has shone

Gwalchmai   74 74 D   J. D. Jones 1827–1870

alternative tune LLANFAIR

IN our darkness light has shone,
Alleluia,
still today the light shines on,
Alleluia;
Word made flesh in human birth,
Alleluia,
Light and Life of all the earth,
Alleluia!

2   Christ the Son incarnate see,
Alleluia,
by whom all things came to be,
Alleluia;
through the world his splendours shine,
Alleluia,
full of grace and truth divine,
Alleluia!

3   All who now in him believe,
Alleluia,
everlasting life receive,
Alleluia;
born of God and in his care,
Alleluia,
we his Name and nature share,
Alleluia!

4   Christ a child on earth appears,
Alleluia,
crown of all creation's years,
Alleluia;
God's eternal Word has come,
Alleluia,
he shall lead his people home,
Alleluia!

18 Not in lordly state

PICARDY 87 87 87

French carol melody in
Chansons Populaires Vol.4, Paris 1860
harmonised by Ralph Vaughan Williams 1872–1958

alternative tune GRAFTON

NOT in lordly state and splendour,
    lofty pomp and high renown;
infant-form his robe most royal,
    lantern-light his only crown;
see the new-born King of glory,
    Lord of all to earth come down!

2 His no rich and storied mansion,
        kingly rule and sceptred sway;
    from his seat in highest heaven
        throned among the beasts he lay;
    see the new-born King of glory
        cradled in his couch of hay!

3 Yet the eye of faith beholds him,
        King above all earthly kings;
    Lord of uncreated ages,
        he whose praise eternal rings;
    see the new-born King of glory
        panoplied by angels' wings!

4 Not in lordly state and splendour,
        lofty pomp and high renown;
    infant-form his robe most royal,
        lantern-light his only crown;
    Christ the new-born King of glory,
        Lord of all to earth come down!

19   O child of Mary, hark to her

THE AULD HOOSE   DCM

Scottish traditional melody
arranged by Lionel Dakers *b.* 1924

alternative tunes FOREST GREEN, KINGSFOLD

O CHILD of Mary, hark to her
   and to the song she sings,
of gold and frankincense and myrrh,
   the shepherds and the kings.
The light of love is in her eyes
   and music on her breath,
that tells of Galilean skies,
   and home, and Nazareth.

2 She sings of sunlight through the door,
   the olive and the vine,
and shavings on the workshop floor
   of resin-scented pine;
of winter stars, and fires alight,
   and bed and hearth and board,
and only sometimes, in the night,
   the shadow of a sword.

3 O sinless child, for sinners born
   to suffering and loss,
the bitter nails, the cruel thorn,
   the darkness and the cross;
no song, since ever time began,
   can tell the path you trod,
O Son of Mary, Son of Man,
   redeeming Son of God.

4 Yet have we songs: no death and grave,
   no cross with all its pains,
can master him who died to save
   and now in glory reigns.
To him, our ever-living Lord,
   new songs are ours to sing:
the crown, the triumph and the sword
   are yours, O Christ our King.

20   O Prince of peace

RECTORY MEADOW   irregular

Erik Routley 1917–1982

1 O Prince of peace whose pro - mised birth the
2 O child who found to lay your head no
3 O Christ whom shep - herds came to find, their
4 O Sa - viour Christ, a - scend - ed Lord, our

an - - gels sang with 'Peace__ on earth',
place__ but in a man - ger bed,
joy____ be ours in heart__ and mind;
ri - - sen Prince of life____ re - stored,

peace be to us and all____ be - side,____
come where our doors stand o - pen wide,____
let grief and care be laid__ a - side,____
our Love who once for sin - ners died,____

peace to us all,_____ *(go to last line)*
peace to us all,_____ peace to the world, *(go to last line)*
peace to us all,_____ peace to the world,
peace to us all,_____ peace to the world,

(3) peace in our homes,____ *(go to last line)*
(4) peace in our homes,____ peace in our hearts,____

all verses

peace to the world_ this Christ - - mas - tide.
peace in our homes_ this Christ - - mas - tide.
peace in our hearts_ this Christ - - mas - tide.
peace with our God__ this Christ - - mas - tide.

Verses 1 to 3 have fewer lines of text than does verse 4. The last line of music is common to all verses and, in the first three verses, the performer is instructed at which point to jump to that last line, omitting the music in between.

21 Peace be yours and dreamless slumber

THANET   8 3 3 6

Melody by Joseph Jowett 1784–1856
in *Musæ Solitariæ* 1823
harmony probably by David Evans 1874–1948

PEACE be yours and dreamless slumber,
heaven's King
come to bring
blessings without number.

2 Helpless now in love's surrender,
by your birth,
child of earth,
emptied of all splendour.

3 Dearest Jesus! So we name you,
born to save;
cross and grave
soon will come to claim you.

4 Then to heaven's throne ascended!
All our tears,
wasted years,
sins and sorrows ended.

5 Sing we then, O Saviour sleeping,
our Noël,
all is well,
in the Father's keeping.

22   See, to us a child is born

INNOCENTS   77 77

The Parish Choir   1850
arranged by W. H. Monk 1823–1889

alternative tunes HARTS, LAUDS (WILSON)

SEE, to us a child is born:
glory breaks on Christmas morn!

2   Now to us a Son is given:
praise to God in highest heaven!

3   On his shoulder rule shall rest:
in him all the earth be blest!

4   Wise and wonderful his Name:
heaven's Lord in human frame!

5   Mighty God, who mercy brings:
Lord of lords and King of kings!

6   Father of eternal days:
every creature sing his praise!

7   Everlasting Prince of peace:
truth and righteousness increase!

8   He shall reign from shore to shore:
Christ is King for evermore!

Two verses of words are apportioned to the tune, which may be performed
with alternate lines of text sung by choir or soloist and by congregation.

23   Stars of heaven, clear and bright

SALZBURG   77 77 D

Jakob Hintze 1622–1702
harmonised by J. S. Bach 1685–1750

alternative tunes ST EDMUND, ST GEORGE'S WINDSOR

STARS of heaven, clear and bright,
shine upon this Christmas night.
Vaster far than midnight skies
are its timeless mysteries.
Trampled earth and stable floor
lift the heart to heaven's door:
God has sent to us his Son,
earth and heaven meet as one.

2   Sleepy sounds of beast and byre
mingle with the angel choir.
Highest heaven bends in awe
where he lies amid the straw,
who from light eternal came
aureoled in candle-flame:
God has sent to us his Son,
earth and heaven meet as one.

3   Wide-eyed shepherds mutely gaze
at the child whom angels praise.
Threefold gifts the wise men bring,
to the infant priest and king;
to the Lord immortal, myrrh
for an earthly sepulchre:
God has sent to us his Son,
earth and heaven meet as one.

4   Heaven of heavens hails his birth,
King of glory, child of earth,
born in flesh to reign on high,
Prince of life to bleed and die.
Throned on Mary's lap he lies,
Lord of all eternities:
God has sent to us his Son,
earth and heaven meet as one.

5   'Glory be to God on high,
peace on earth,' the angels cry.
Ancient enmities at rest,
ransomed, reconciled and blest,
in the peace of Christ we come,
come we joyful, come we home:
God has sent to us his Son,
earth and heaven meet as one.

24 The darkness turns to dawn

SANDYS   SM

from W. Sandys's *Christmas Carols* 1833

alternative tunes CARLISLE, ST THOMAS

THE darkness turns to dawn,
  the dayspring shines from heaven,
for unto us a child is born,
  to us a son is given.

2 The Son of God most high,
     before all else began,
   a virgin's son behold him lie,
     the new-born Son of Man.

3 God's Word of truth and grace
     made flesh with us to dwell;
   the brightness of the Father's face,
     the child Emmanuel.

4 How rich his heavenly home!
     How poor his human birth!
   As mortal man he stoops to come,
     the light and life of earth.

5 A servant's form, a slave,
     the Lord consents to share;
   our sin and shame, our cross and grave,
     he bows himself to bear.

6 Obedient and alone
     upon that cross to die,
   and then to share the Father's throne
     in majesty on high.

7 And still God sheds abroad
     that love so strong to send
   a Saviour, who is Christ the Lord,
     whose reign shall never end.

25   The hush of midnight here below

REPTON   86 88 6

Arranged from the oratorio *Judith* by
C. H. H. Parry 1848–1918
arranged for manuals only by Michael Fleming *b.* 1928

THE hush of midnight here below,
the shining stars above,
a night of wonder long ago
when in the stable lantern's glow
is born God's gift of love.

2 To all the waiting world belongs
the child now brought to birth,
who comes to right our human wrongs,
his praises told in angel songs,
proclaiming peace on earth.

3 Judæan shepherds stand in awe,
in wide-eyed wonder dumb,
to see amid the stable's straw,
fulfilling all the ancient law,
the Lamb of God is come.

4 The kings of earth in homage ride
to where the child is born;
a King to whom a star shall guide,
whose throne is at the Father's side,
his crown a crown of thorn.

5 This child, whose birth the angels tell,
whose death our life restored,
by whom at last shall all be well,
is God with us, Immanuel,
our Saviour, Christ the Lord.

26 The King of glory comes to earth

LADYWELL   DCM

W. H. Ferguson 1872–1950

alternative tune KINGSFOLD

THE King of glory comes to earth
from God the Father given,
the heralds of his royal birth
the angel host of heaven;
his kingly robe the swathing bands,
his homage Mary's gaze,
beyond the stars his kingdom stands
to everlasting days.

2   The King of glory comes unknown,
the infant Lord of all;
a mother's lap his only throne,
his state a cattle stall.
Before their naked new-born King
the ox and ass are dumb,
while countless choirs of angels sing
to see his kingdom come.

3   The King of glory comes to die
in poverty and scorn,
upon a donkey riding by
to claim a crown of thorn.
Creation's Lord of time and space
is come to meet his hour,
his triumph-song the word of grace,
and love his only power.

4   The King of glory comes in peace,
and hope is ours again,
as life and love and joy increase
and faith and freedom reign.
The Child of all our Christmas songs,
his cross and passion past,
will right the sum of human wrongs
and bring us home at last.

27   Through centuries long

HANOVER   10 10 11 11

A Supplement to the New Version 1708
descant by Alan Gray 1855–1935

The descant may be sung by sopranos in verse 6, the main melody being sung in unison

alternative tunes OLD 104th, PADERBORN

THROUGH centuries long the prophets of old
in story and song this promise foretold:
a Saviour anointed, a Sovereign supreme,
divinely appointed to rule and redeem.

2   In judgment and peace his power shall be shown,
his kingdom increase, his justice be known;
from nation to nation his reign shall extend
the hope of salvation and life without end.

3   He comes not in state with sceptre and crown,
with panoply great of rank or renown,
but choosing in weakness, his glory put by,
majestic in meekness, to serve and to die.

4   In mercy he came our burden to bear,
our sorrow and shame, our guilt and despair;
an outcast and stranger, he carried our loss
from Bethlehem's manger to Calvary's cross.

5   He rose from the grave, exalted again,
almighty to save, immortal to reign;
let sorrows be ended and joy be restored
for Christ is ascended, for Jesus is Lord!

6   Then honour his Name, rejoice at his birth,
his wonders proclaim through all the wide earth!
The child of our story in Bethlehem's stall
is reigning in glory, our God over all.

28   To this our world of time and space

Cornwall   88 6 88 6   S. S. Wesley   1810–1876

alternative tune   WELLSHIRE

TO this our world of time and space,
a destined hour, a chosen place,
   our Saviour Christ has come:
let earth and sky alike bow down
before his everlasting crown,
   the Lord himself has come!

2   To this our world his hands had made,
in human form and flesh arrayed,
   our Saviour Christ has come:
the light of God's eternal light
to end our fallen nature's night,
   the Lord himself has come!

3   To this our world, to seek and save,
to crib and crown, to cross and grave,
   our Saviour Christ has come:
the promised gift of God above,
amazing grace, immortal love,
   the Lord himself has come!

4   To this our world of joy and pain,
to die for us and rise again,
   our Saviour Christ has come:
to die for us and rise again,
and over all the earth to reign,
   the Lord himself has come!

Text © Copyright Timothy Dudley-Smith in Europe (including UK and Ireland) and Africa,
and in the rest of the world © 1996 by Hope Publishing Company

29   **Where do Christmas songs begin?**

St Edmund   77 77 D   Charles Steggall 1826–1905

alternative tunes   SALZBURG,   ST GEORGE'S WINDSOR

WHERE do Christmas songs begin?
By the stable of an inn
where the song of hosts on high
mingled with a baby's cry.
There, for joy and wonder, smiled
man and maid and holy child.
Christmas songs begin with them:
sing the songs of Bethlehem!

2 Who is this, whose human birth
here proclaims him child of earth?
He it is who formed the skies,
saw the new-made stars arise:
life immortal, light divine,
blinking in the candle-shine;
born our darkness to dispel,
God with us, Emmanuel!

3 Only love can answer why
he should come to grieve and die,
share on earth our pain and loss,
bear for us the bitter cross.
Love is come to seek and save,
life to master death and grave,
so in Christ is all restored,
risen and redeeming Lord!

4 Praise we then, in Christmas songs,
him to whom all praise belongs.
Hear the angel host reply,
'Glory be to God on high,
joy and peace to mortals given,
peace on earth and peace with heaven!'
join we now, as one with them:
sing the songs of Bethlehem!

30   Within a crib my Saviour lay

EWHURST   88 87

C. J. Allen 1886–1973

WITHIN a crib my Saviour lay,
a wooden manger filled with hay,
come down for love on Christmas Day:
  all glory be to Jesus!

2 Upon a cross my Saviour died,
   to ransom sinners crucified,
   his loving arms still open wide:
     all glory be to Jesus!

3 A victor's crown my Saviour won,
   his work of love and mercy done,
   the Father's high-ascended Son:
     all glory be to Jesus!

INDEX OF TUNES